**Anne Ablay
Peter Goulden
Neil Nuckley
Peter Toft**

Oxford University Press

ABOUT THIS BOOK

This book will help you to think about the future as you design and make things. Why do we design and make, though? Well, there are at least three answers to this question.

- Sometimes we design and make something to *solve a problem*.
- Sometimes we design and make because we see an opportunity to *produce something useful* or valuable.
- And sometimes we design and make *for fun*, just because we feel like it.

You can do all three as you work through this book.
As you do you will need to work in certain ways including:

- thinking hard about a task or a problem;
- finding out or doing *research*;
- developing ideas;
- making;
- testing what you have made.

The book is divided into three sections.

- CHANGES looks at the way we might live and what we might wear in the future.
- ENVIRONMENTS deals with where we might live.
- MESSAGES looks at how we might communicate with one another.

In each section you will find a number of topics. From each topic you will learn certain ideas and facts. You will also be asked to do certain tasks. Please note that you must always check with your teacher before starting these. To help you to recognise the different tasks, we have used symbols:

- ★ means *do* something
- ■ means here is a useful *hint*
- ◆ means you need to *find something out* or do research
- ● means you are asked to think about or *discuss* something in class
- ▲ means you need to *test* something

Designing and making things are important. So are thinking about and planning for the future. But these are not the only reasons for this book. Designing and making things can be great fun. We hope you enjoy having such fun with the help of this book.

Anne Ablay   Peter Goulden   Neil Nuckley   Peter Toft

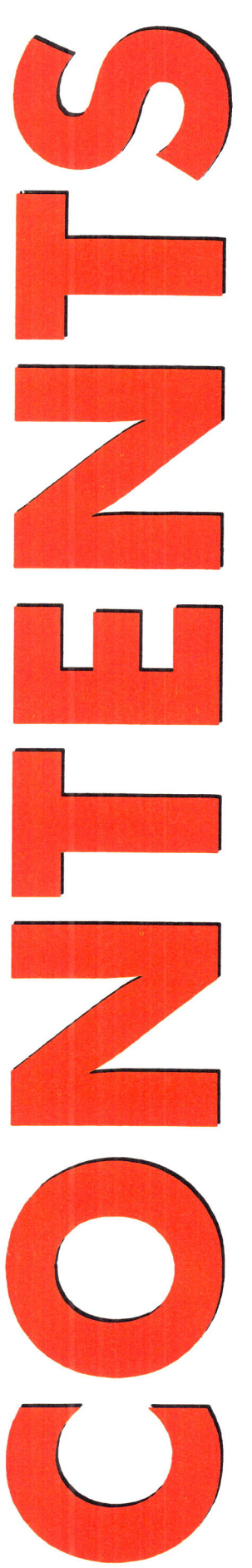

CHANGES

- 6 Times are changing
- 8 A crystal clear future?
- 10 Future fashion
- 12 What to wear and where to wear it
- 17 Putting on a 2020 show
- 20 Getting the show on the road

ENVIRONMENTS

- 24 Where do we go from here?
- 26 Hostile environments
- 28 Homes and environments
- 34 Construction techniques
- 36 Into space
- 38 To the planets

MESSAGES

- 42 Satellite communication
- 44 A future communicator
- 46 We can change the future

- 48 Index

forecasts

Fashion

Communication

signals

leisure

co-ordin

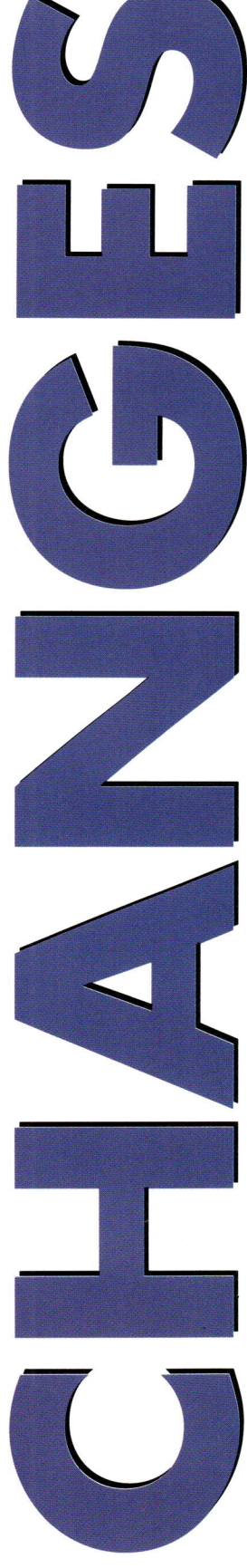

CHANGES

This section is about the way we live, the clothes we wear, and how fashions change. You will be asked to think about the future, especially about clothes. You will also be able to design and make some **futuristic** clothes and to act out a show using the clothes as props.

TIMES ARE CHANGING

Who knows what the future will be like? Will the world be controlled by robots? Will we live on other planets? We do not know anything about the future for certain but we can be fairly sure that things will be different from how they are now. How do you think things will be different? Try thinking about *change*.

FASHION

◆ Look at what people wear now. How is it different from two years ago, or ten, or even fifty?

● How do fashions change? Why do you think they change? Discuss this with a friend or parent.

◆ In the past most clothes were made from *naturally occurring* materials. Recently many of these have been replaced with *synthetic materials*. Find out what *synthetic* means. Look for examples of clothes made from synthetic materials. What was the *source* of these synthetic materials?

COMMUNICATION

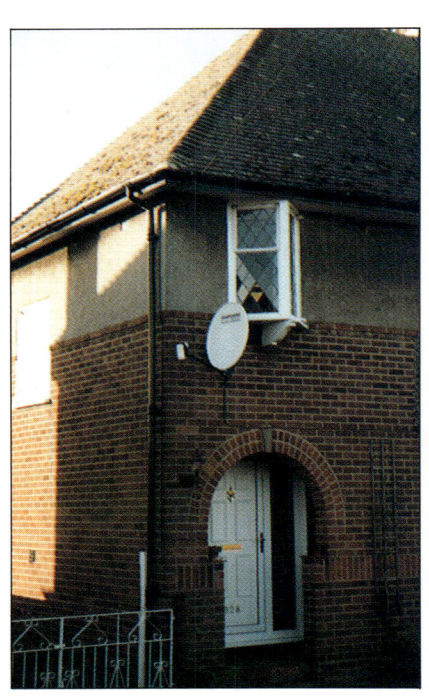

Speed of communication is important in the modern world as we need to send information from place to place as quickly as possible.

◆ Find an adult who is used to receiving information from one of these: *a portable telephone; a computer; a digital watch; CEEFAX*. Ask these questions.

What did you feel like when you first used this device?
How did you receive the information before you used the device?
Have things changed for better or worse?

TRANSPORT

In 1987 there were 22,200,000 cars in the United Kingdom. That is roughly one car for every 3.4 people. Yet in 1957 there were only 7,500,000 cars.

◆ Find out how road transport has changed in the last thirty years.

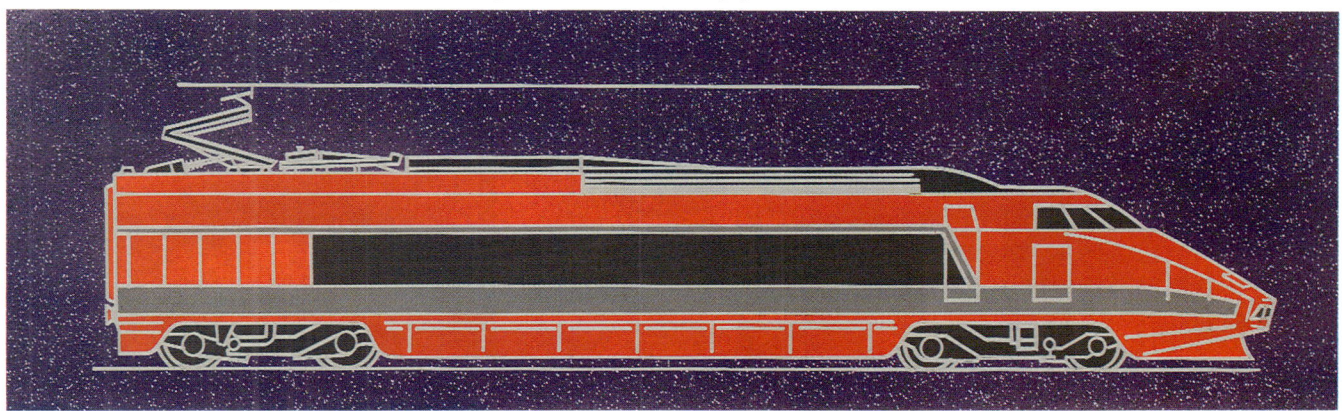

MONEY

Money comes in many different styles. There are coins, notes, cheques, and other things that represent money like credit cards. Then there are things we exchange for money and use in the future instead of money, like return train tickets or bus passes.

◆ Find out about automatic banking machines. What do you need to make them work? How can they tell that users are genuine and not thieves?

A CRYSTAL CLEAR FUTURE?

"As I look into my crystal ball, the future is very misty . . . but look, the mist clears. I see the world of 2020. It is clean and healthy. Pollution has been wiped out. Cars do not crowd the roads . . . public transport is fast and efficient. People have lots of free time which they use for leisure. Most work done by people involves thinking about and looking after other people."

"All other work is done by computer controlled *superbos*. They work non-stop and are guided by advanced *hyperchips*. The superbos make the country wealthy and all people share in this wealth. They are paid in Eurocredits."

"Every adult gets 800 Eurocredits per month plus 200 for each of the first two children. Families with more than two children do not get any extra. You can swop Eurocredits for lots of different services. The services are usually sold in *megamarts*, large shops that sell everything. Style and fashions are very personal. Clothes are made up by the customers. They simply choose the parts they like such as sleeves, collars, bodice, etc. then join them together. No two people are dressed alike. The crystal ball is misting again. I hope this has helped to show you how the world might look in 2020."

- The crystal ball has shown a very pleasant view of the future, but perhaps we will not solve all our problems by 2020. Perhaps they will get worse or new problems may arise. What do *you* think the world will be like? Discuss this with a friend then write an account, illustrated if you like, of what *you* think the world will be like in 2020.

THINKING ABOUT 2020

● Try to imagine what life will be like. Some entries in a diary are shown below. They might help you to imagine a typical day in 2020.

What will a shop look like?
What will it sell?
How will customers pay?
What might a Eurocredit look like?
Can you design a Eurocredit?
What is a personal communicator?
What might it look like?
What will people wear?

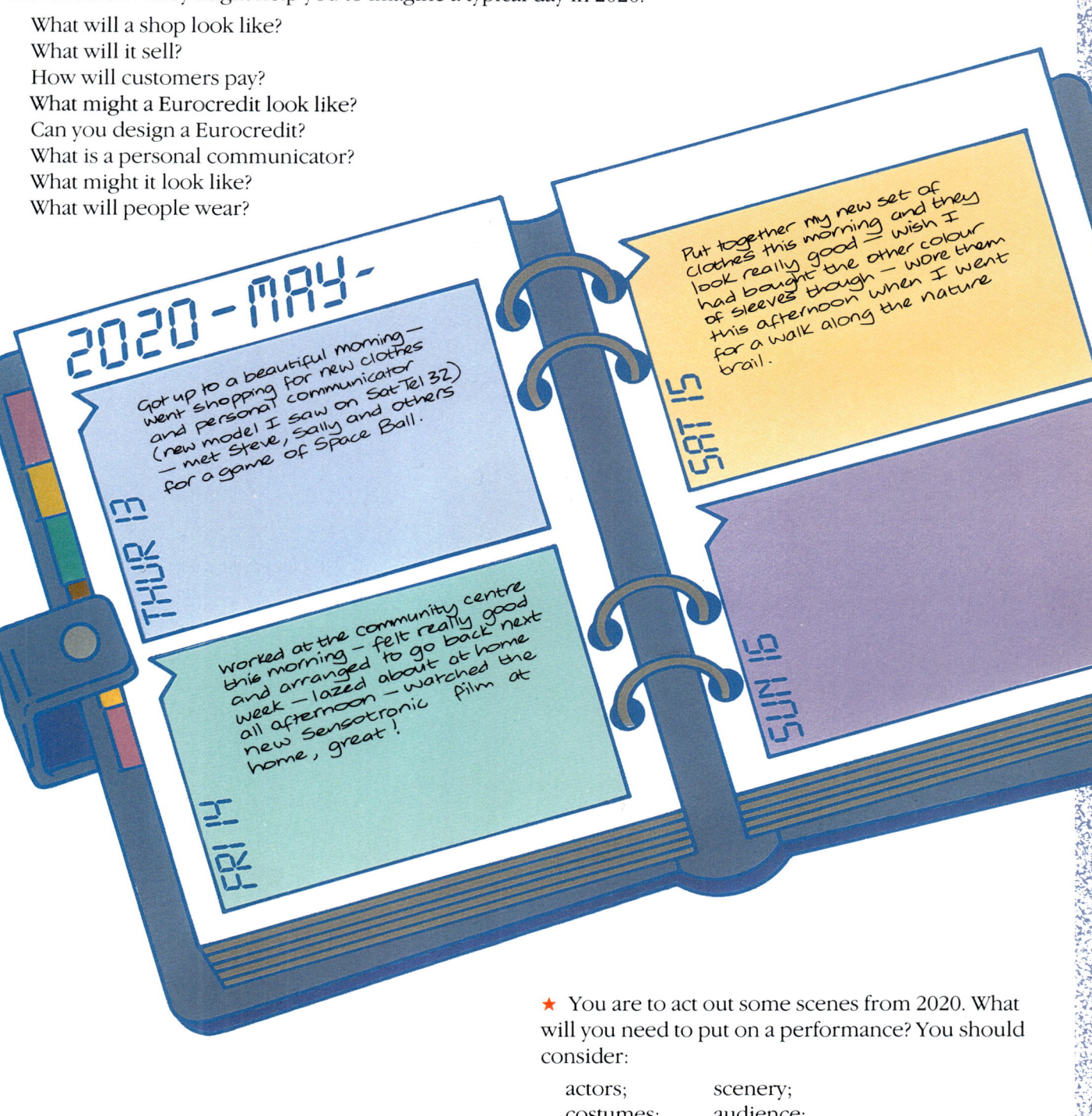

2020 — MAY —

THUR 13 — Got up to a beautiful morning — went shopping for new clothes and personal communicator (new model I saw on SatTel 32) — met Steve, Sally and others for a game of Space Ball.

FRI 14 — Worked at the community centre this morning — felt really good and arranged to go back next week — lazed about at home all afternoon — watched the new Sensotronic film at home, great!

SAT 15 — Put together my new set of clothes this morning and they look really good — wish I had bought the other colour of sleeves though — wore them this afternoon when I went for a walk along the nature trail.

★ You are to act out some scenes from 2020. What will you need to put on a performance? You should consider:

actors;   scenery;
costumes; audience;
props;   space.

Turn the page for some ideas to help you solve these problems.

FUTURE FASHION

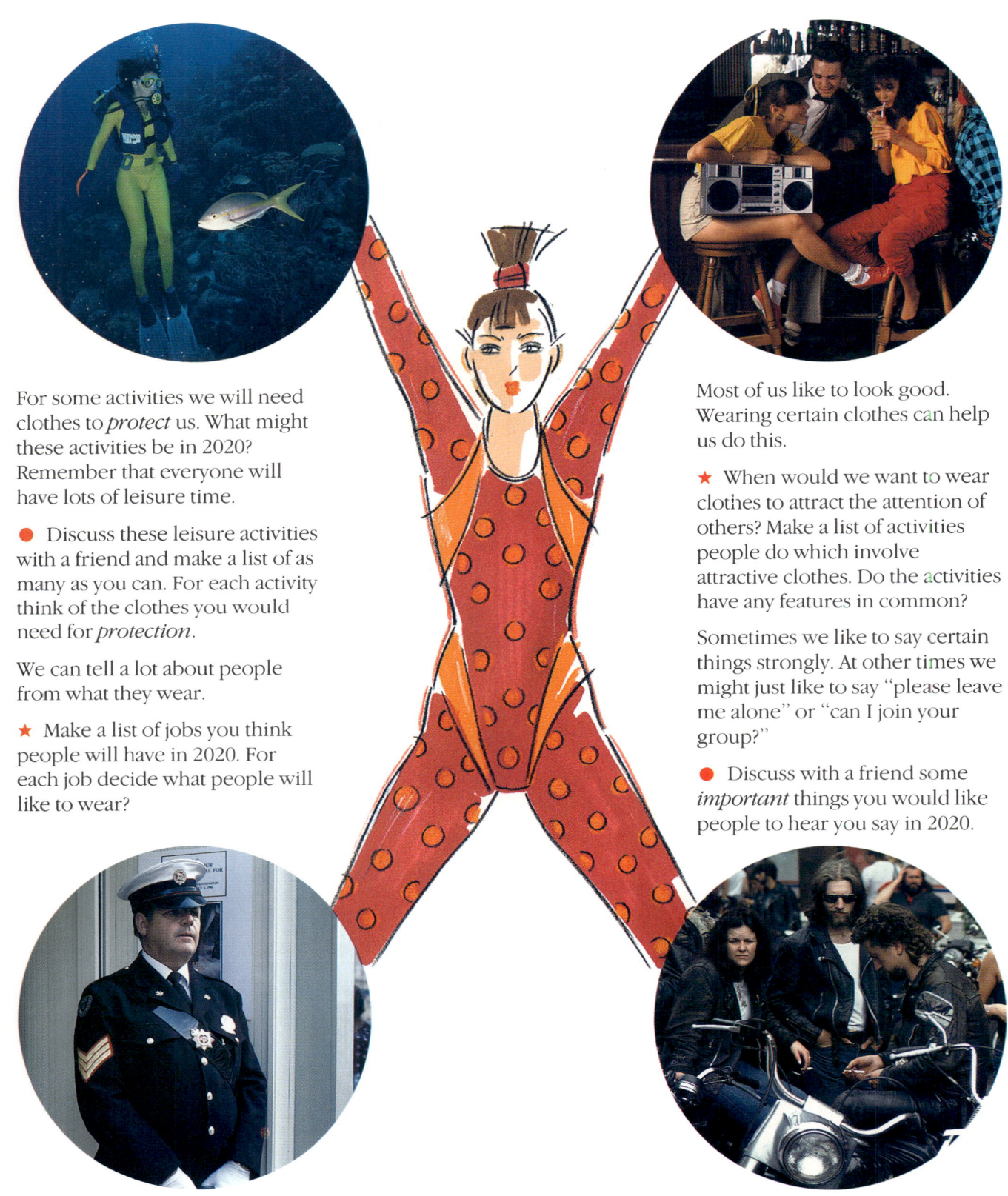

For some activities we will need clothes to *protect* us. What might these activities be in 2020? Remember that everyone will have lots of leisure time.

● Discuss these leisure activities with a friend and make a list of as many as you can. For each activity think of the clothes you would need for *protection*.

We can tell a lot about people from what they wear.

★ Make a list of jobs you think people will have in 2020. For each job decide what people will like to wear?

Most of us like to look good. Wearing certain clothes can help us do this.

★ When would we want to wear clothes to attract the attention of others? Make a list of activities people do which involve attractive clothes. Do the activities have any features in common?

Sometimes we like to say certain things strongly. At other times we might just like to say "please leave me alone" or "can I join your group?"

● Discuss with a friend some *important* things you would like people to hear you say in 2020.

FASHION FORECAST

Let us think again about acting out scenes from 2020. The tasks on the last two pages will have helped you to think about the clothes people might wear. Think about the points below.

- How might clothes be different in 2020?
  What will the materials be like?
  What styles might be fashionable?
  Will people all wear the same things?
  Who will decide how clothes look?

Now think about the reasons why clothes are worn. Clothes have many different purposes. They are designed differently for each main purpose. Clothes can:

keep us warm;
keep us cool;
frighten us;
make us attractive;
be fun.

SIGNALS

Clothes can be a reflection of your personality or job. They can also reflect the personality you would like to be.

★ Why dress up for a disco or a party? Make a list of as many reasons as you can.

Clothes can 'speak' for you without being able to speak themselves. They give visual signals about you. These signals help others to make judgements about you.

★ Collect photographs from magazines of unusual clothes which give signals about people. Stick them in your design book.

WHAT TO WEAR AND WHERE TO WEAR IT

This section considers some ways to make clothing for different parts of the body.

★ Study the next few pages and then create an item of costume for part of your body which would be suitable for the year 2020.

DESIGN TASK: AHEAD OF THE REST

★ You can make a basic helmet shape by moulding papier mâché around a balloon. Papier mâché becomes very hard if you use enough layers of paper (not too many) and leave it for long enough to set. Try adding extra detail with card or other materials.

 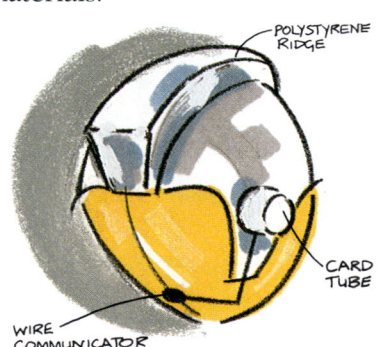 

★ When used to improve our eyesight spectacles are very *functional* but they can also be very fashionable. For example sunglasses protect us from glare but they are often worn to create an image. They can make us mysterious, usually because others cannot see our eyes. Try making a pair of *Hi-Tec Specs*. If you use your imagination you can create some fantastic 2020 'specs'. Try making a card mock-up first to see if your ideas work. When you are satisfied with the design you could make your 'specs' in acrylic sheet, rigid polystyrene or even polycarbonate (expensive!).

★ Why not create headbands to set off that 21st century hairstyle? Take a look at some science fiction comics for ideas. Could you make your helmet, 'specs' or headband flash electronically? Try using flashing light-emitting diodes (LEDs) See page 15 for more information.

DESIGN TASK: IT'S THE TOPS

★ Try making a top for your arms and shoulders. Here are some ideas.

It might be easier to start with an old garment like a shirt, vest, T-shirt or jacket. You can then add details to get the effects you want. If you are feeling really adventurous you could make up a garment from a pattern or from your own design. You may not consider a plastic bin liner to be very stylish yet you could use one as the basis for a Hi-Tec garment. Such plastic sheeting is a fairly recent material for clothes and still looks very unusual. A T-shirt with a triangle motif added can be worn with a belt to give it more shape. The motif can be made from coloured plastic sheet.

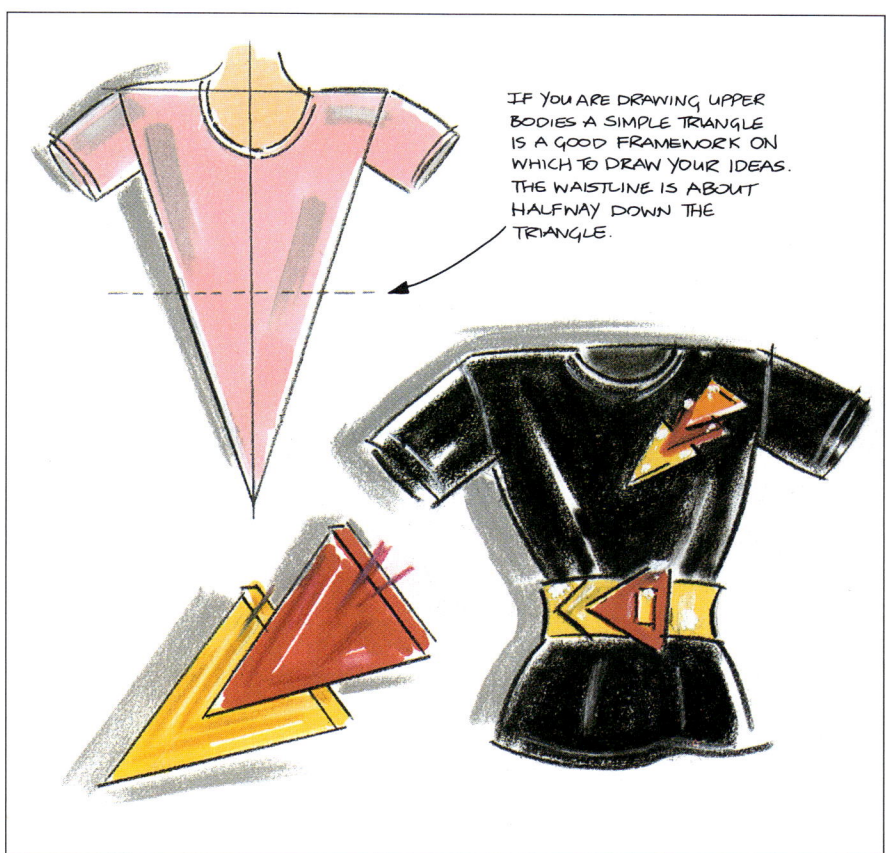

IF YOU ARE DRAWING UPPER BODIES A SIMPLE TRIANGLE IS A GOOD FRAMEWORK ON WHICH TO DRAW YOUR IDEAS. THE WAISTLINE IS ABOUT HALFWAY DOWN THE TRIANGLE.

A belt can be made from various materials. How many suitable materials can you think of? The buckle could be designed to be the same as the T-shirt motif or you could link a series of shapes in some way to make a flexible belt.

◆ Try to find out the name of the first plastic used in clothes. Which of your clothes contain plastic materials? How are these materials different from a plastic bin liner?

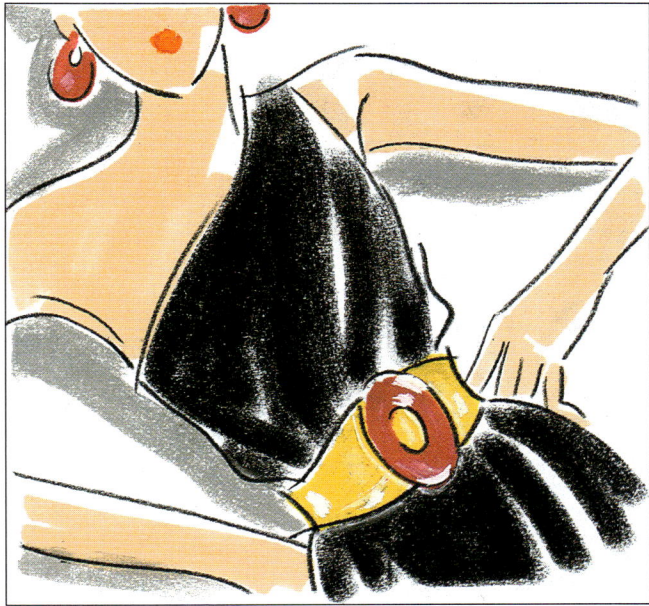

Which parts of the bin liner will you remove for your arms and head? How can you make the shape look really stylish? What about an 'off the shoulder' look or adding some detail?

13

DESIGN TASK: COLD SHOULDER

★ Chunky wrist bracelets can create a 'tough' image. You can make them easily in card or acrylic, or less easily in metal. A less aggressive image can be created by a different style and position for the arm bands.

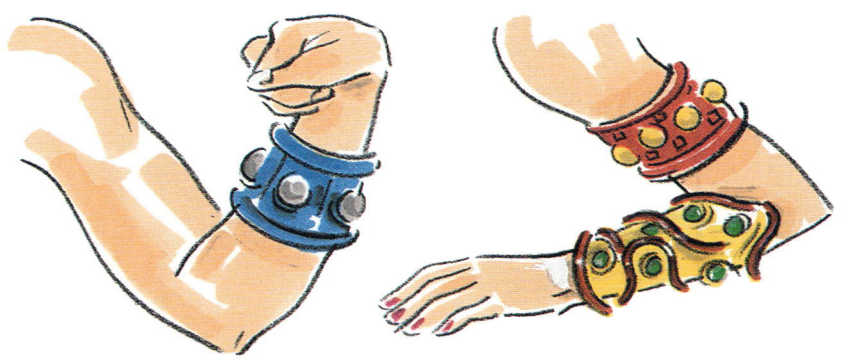

Shoulders can be made to look very spectacular and dramatic. Shoulder dress is often used to show the status of the wearer.

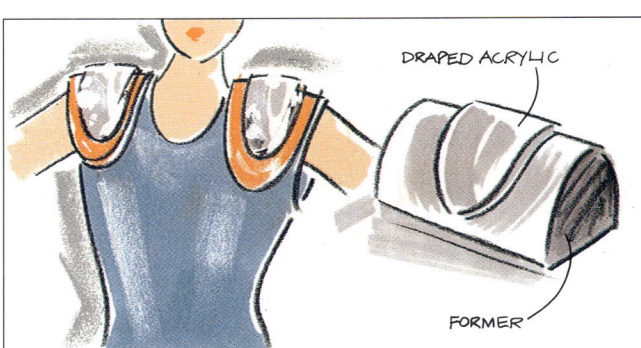

These shoulder pads could be made from various materials. Try heating shaped acrylic in an oven and draping it around a *former*.

Sleeves and shoulder protection are important in many different types of costume.

A combination of materials might be best for these shoulder pads. Could metal be used? What about leather and fabrics?

◆ Find the History of Costume section of your library. Read about how arm and shoulder decoration has changed through the ages. Choose some examples from history and work out how they showed the status of their wearers. Make notes and sketches in your design book.

This style on the right suggests something padded or soft, but it could be made of vacuum-formed sections joined together.

● Discuss ways of joining together such sections so that they allow the body to move.

DESIGN TASK: LIGHT IT UP

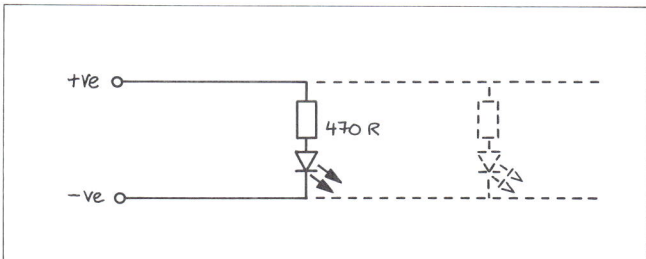

★ Electronic jewellery can be quite exciting. You can use an LED in a brooch or bracelet. LEDs or *light-emitting diodes* generally come in red, yellow and green colours. If you connect one into a circuit it will light up. Other LEDs can be added as the dotted lines show.

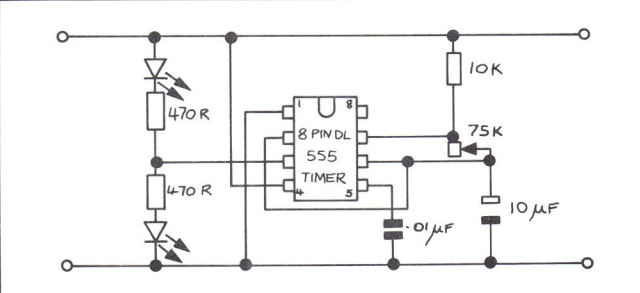

If you want your light(s) to flash you will need to connect up the circuit as shown above.

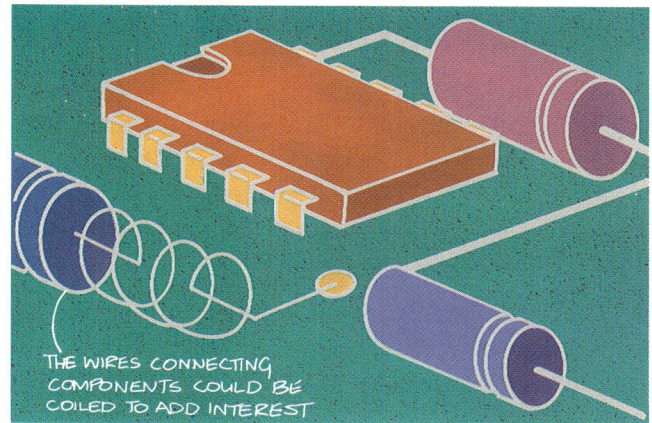

The wires connecting components could be coiled to add interest

You can make these circuits compact enough to hide behind a piece of jewellery but the battery may need to be fixed into a pocket. Or your could leave the electronics exposed as part of the overall effect.

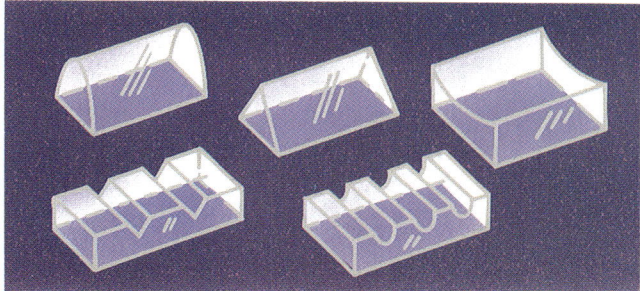

Lenses made from shaped and polished acrylic can give interesting effects when placed over the top of LEDs.

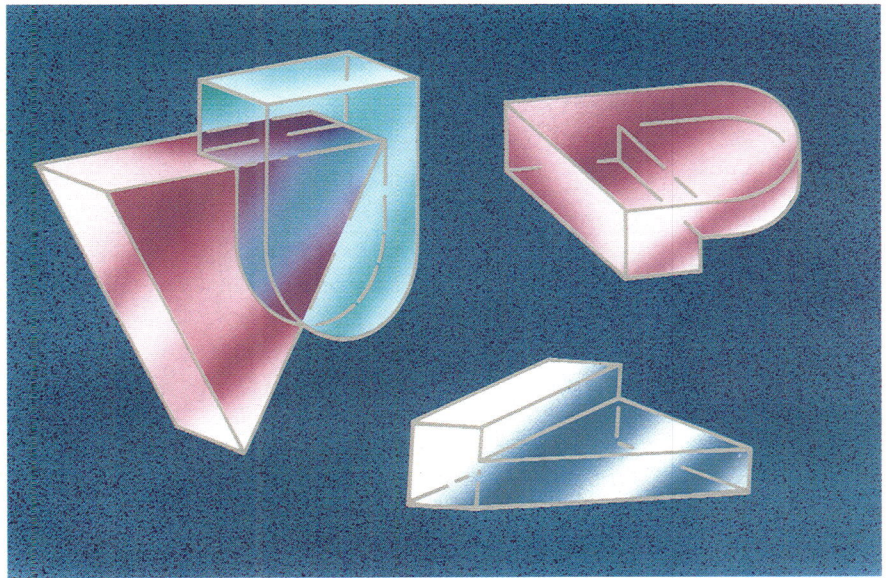

These brooches or badges could have interchangeable pieces. You could change their appearance to suit your mood or match them to different clothes.

These panels could hinge outwards to transform the appearance and reveal something like an LED.

EXTRA BITS

There might be some accessories which no self-respecting 2020 citizen would be seen without. What kinds of things might people carry around in 2020? Think about the ideas discussed below.

DESIGN TASK: PERSONAL ENTERTAINMENT

Electronic devices are getting smaller and smaller. Today you can even buy calculators which fit into wrist-watches. How small might personal entertainment devices be in 2020? Will a compact disc unit, radio, or TV be as small as a wrist-watch or a piece of jewellery?

★ Design and make a model of a 2020 miniature personal entertainment device which can be worn on the body.

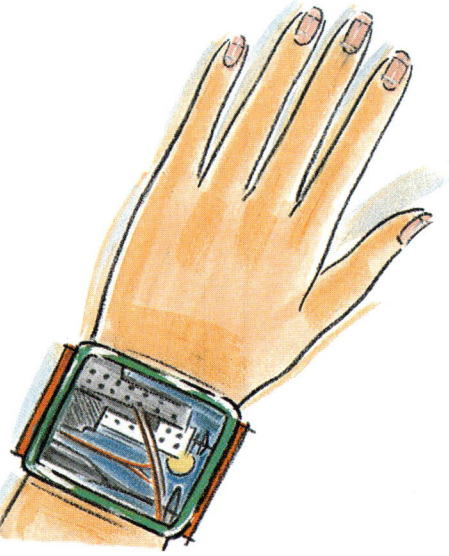

DESIGN TASK: SURVIVAL PACK

● Think about these 2020 products:

   high protein food in tiny tablets;
   small portable heaters to warm the body or food;
   very lightweight transportable shelters.

Could these be carried in a *belt* in 2020?
When would they be needed?
What other special equipment will be needed to help a person survive?

★ Make a survival pack to hold some of these items. Design it to be worn as a belt.

LEISURE

Can you design a new game for the 21st century with your friends? How do you think *technology* will change the way we play games. Imagine a game of *Space Ball*. To make a ball move in a game we have to kick it, throw it, hit it or bounce it. Perhaps in 2020 game balls will move by themselves. If the ball moves by itself what does the player do to play the game?

★ Design such a game, plan the rules and make the equipment and clothing.

PUTTING ON A 2020 SHOW

To put on a dramatic performance you need:
- *actors*;
- something to *say*;
- *space* to perform;
- *costumes*;
- *scenery*;
- *props* (extra things to help the actor);
- and last, but not least, *an audience*.

The last few pages have given you some ideas for costumes and props. Here are some ideas for producing a play. Remember that each member of your team will have a different role.

WHAT ARE YOU GOING TO SAY?

★ Start with a short plan. For example imagine that you are going to watch the new *sensotronic* movie with a friend. The scene starts as you get off the hover-rail. What happens? Well it's up to you, but a *story-board* might help. A story-board uses pictures to devise the main events. The first could be of two people leaving the hover-rail.

What would they do next? Go to the robo-burger bar? Watch the holographic shop displays? Or simply go to the senso-cinema? Whatever happens is drawn onto the next board. Draw a board for each major event. Be careful though because if you have too many you may not be able to produce all the scenery.

IMPROVISATION

One way of acting out your play is to *improvise*. As long as you know roughly how the story develops each actor can respond naturally to what the other says. This can often be very effective and you will not need to learn lots of lines.

WRITE IT DOWN

★ Another way is to write down all that the actors say and do. This means that each actor knows exactly how to perform but it will mean that everyone has to learn their lines properly.

TAKE THREE

★ If you are to perform the play before an audience then get lots of practice. Even if you are improvising, such practice, or rehearsal will allow you to try out different ideas.

Ask yourself these questions.
- Will the play be better with props and scenery?
- How many actors do you need?
- What space do you need?
- Do you need an audience?
- Will the play have to be advertised?
- Will tickets be necessary?

If yes is the answer to any of these questions, how will you provide what is needed?

PROPS

MAKE-UP BOX MODIFIED TO APPEAR LIKE A COMMUNICATOR

★ Actors often use objects in a play. These are *props*. Certain 2020 props may be familiar to us today. If so you might be able to borrow them for your play. Other props may have to be made.

A prop does not have to work exactly like the original but it must look effective enough for the audience to believe it is real. Often props can be made from 'throw-away' materials.

SCENERY

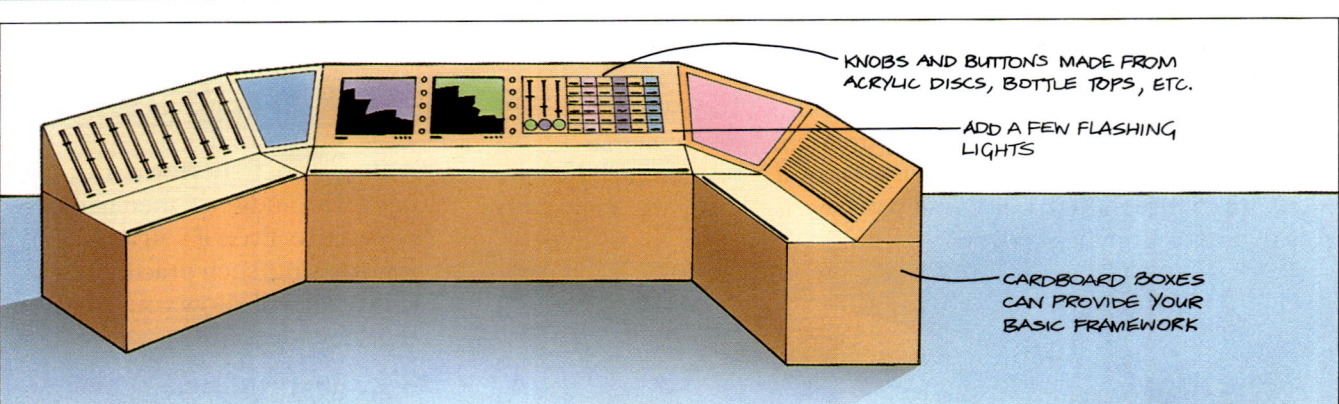

KNOBS AND BUTTONS MADE FROM ACRYLIC DISCS, BOTTLE TOPS, ETC.

ADD A FEW FLASHING LIGHTS

CARDBOARD BOXES CAN PROVIDE YOUR BASIC FRAMEWORK

★ Like props, scenery doesn't have to be complicated. It simply needs to create the right atmosphere. Often just inviting the audience to use their imaginations will do. You could create a control console from cardboard boxes and add detail using other 'throw-away' materials.

WOODEN FRAME

HARDBOARD, PAPER, CARDBOARD, ETC.

A *flat* can give the impression of a background. It is a simple wooden frame covered with something cheap like paper, card, or hardboard and then painted.

Try creating a scene using *back projection*. Here you project a suitable slide or even a movie onto a large white sheet of cloth. The audience can see the image on the other side.

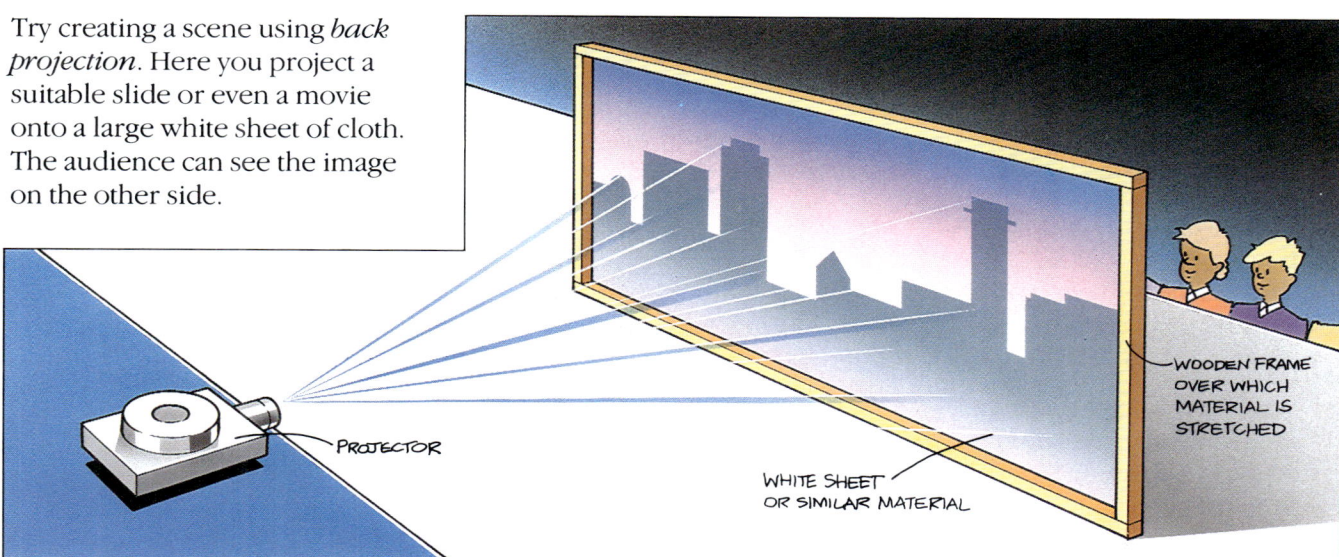

LIGHTING

★ Many schools have proper stage lighting which you might be able to use. Ask your drama teacher. You can achieve many exciting effects by the careful placing of lamps. The colour of the light can be changed by adding filters to the lamps. This helps to create the right atmosphere. What effects do you think the following kinds of filter might have: red; blue; pink; green?

Lighting a subject from behind gives a sinister, almost ghostly appearance and the features are 'lost'. Lighting from the sides gives a more natural appearance although other effects can be achieved. Lighting from below gives the subject a very frightening appearance. Try it yourself using a torch!

GETTING THE SHOW ON THE ROAD

ADVERTISING

★ You may need to advertise your play to attract an audience.
● Discuss the following with your classmates then design and produce posters, tickets, and programmes for the play.

- Who do you want to attract?
- What do you expect them to see?
- Who is performing?
- Who wrote the play?
- When are you performing?
- Where will it be performed?
- How much will it cost?

TICKETS

Tickets will of course be much smaller than programmes and posters. However, they should hold much of the same information.

When designing tickets and posters, think about these important points:

- lettering style;
- the position of the lettering;
- other graphics;
- colour.

Will the money from ticket sales cover your costs? Do you want to make a profit? What would you do with any profit? You could give to charity or buy equipment or finance your next play.

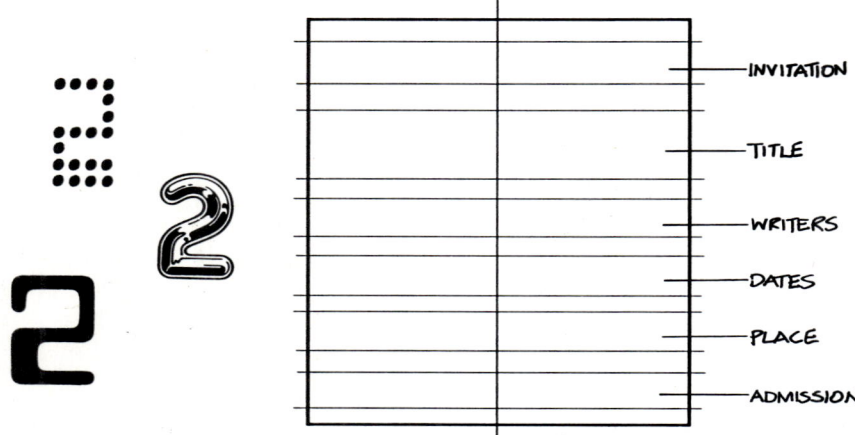

These lettering styles look futuristic. You could use styles like them for your design. Plan out the main areas of your design in pencil first. Varying the letter sizes will add interest and help draw attention to particular parts of the design.

A centre line might help you keep your work neat. Don't be afraid to place things off-centre though as this can often look more interesting.

GRAPHICS

Graphics are very important in advertising. Careful use of *images* will help you give clear ideas about your play. The same images can be repeated on tickets, posters, and programmes. Choose images which make a *visual impact*, images that stand out. You can get ideas for this by looking at science fiction comics or computer games.

PROGRAMMES

Your programme might contain:
- an introduction, explaining why the play is being performed;
- the order of performance;
- a cast list;
- thanks to those people who have made the performance possible;
- credits for scenery, costumes, props, advertising, lighting script, etc.

SHAPE

Most tickets are rectangles of card. Perhaps you could devise something a little more unusual than this. Remember that a ticket will not contain all the information on your poster, just enough to remind people of the name of the play and when and where it will be performed.

materials

Energy

Recycling

Shelter

location

essential

This section is about the houses in which we might live in the future. It looks at different places we might build them on earth or in space. Problems of building are examined and ways to overcome them suggested. You will be able to design and make a model of a future home and other things linked to houses.

ENVIRONMENTS

Food

artificial

WHERE DO WE GO FROM HERE?

People have basic needs which alter very little. For example we all need *food*, *warmth*, *clothing* and *shelter* no matter which part of the world we live in. In modern Britain we take for granted that our basic needs will be met. For the majority of people in this country, food, warmth, clothes, and shelter are available.

For example we don't usually have droughts which seriously affect farming or earthquakes which destroy houses. Certain things could make us re-think the places we live in. Pollution of the earth and atmosphere may become so serious that our lives will be badly affected.

World population is growing at an alarming speed and overcrowding may force us to look for more living space. There are places on earth where, at present, we wouldn't dream of living. Living in space, or on another planet, may soon become possible or maybe we will simply make do with what we have already.

What do you think about these ideas? Read on to develop your own views and try out some of your own ideas.

HOSTILE ENVIRONMENTS

◀ Overcrowding in some towns and cities is a serious problem. We all need space to live in. Without this space we feel cramped and uneasy. This can affect the way we get on with others.

Modern science and technology have helped people to transform areas of our planet. Dry, infertile deserts can be made green and pleasant. Areas once under the sea can be reclaimed and used. ▼

All over the world people have built shelters to live in. Many things affect the style of these shelters. Each area or environment presents its own problems.

Geology What is the surface of the land like? How will it affect the way house builders use materials?

Materials What materials are available in the area? How useful are they?

Climate What is the weather like?

Self-sufficiency Can people co-operate with others to provide food, warmth, clothing and shelter? Do small groups have to provide everything for themselves?

Finance How much money do people have to pay for their shelter? Can they borrow? Can they use cheap materials or building methods?

Use Who will use the shelter? What will they expect to do in it?

HOMES AND ENVIRONMENTS

DESIGN TASK: DWELLINGS

★ You can try this project on your own or as part of a team. Design and make a model of a dwelling for two adults and two children. The dwelling must be suitable for *one* of the five 'difficult' environments described in the next pages. For this project models of these environments will need to be made in boxes like the one shown opposite. You may need to make your own before starting your dwelling.

Each box will contain a different *base* material. This will represent the *geology* of the area. The geology will affect the way you build your dwelling and how you fix it to the ground.

Your dwelling must enable the occupants to be self-sufficient – that is they must produce their own *power* and *food*. As you are only making a model these systems do not have to work exactly.

At the end of the project you need to present the following for assessment:
1 a research folder containing the sketches you made of alternative ideas when you were developing your design;
2 a model dwelling made to a high standard;
3 a written or taped account of what you think it would be like to live in your dwelling in its environment.

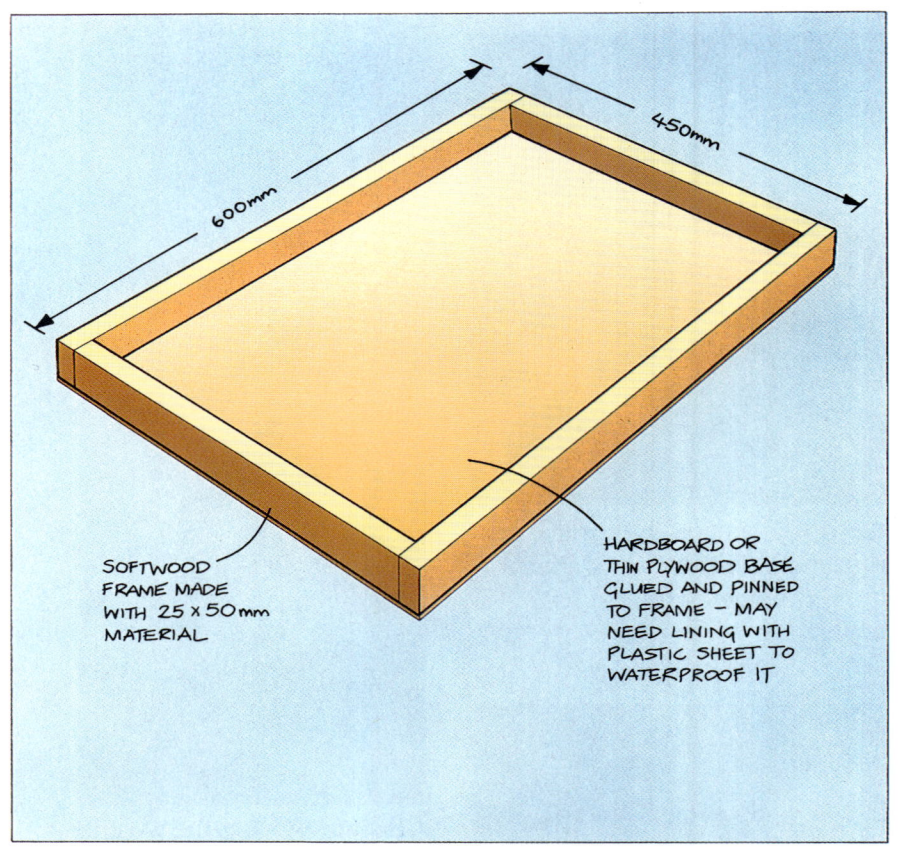

RESEARCH (1)

◆ Your first task will be to find out how *power can be produced from natural sources*. Possible sources are shown here. How do you think they work?

How is electricity produced in this system?

How do these solar collectors work?

What are the drawbacks of using wave power to produce electricity?

How can waste products be used to make power?

RESEARCH (2)

◆ Your second task will be to find out about the *area you will design your dwelling for*. This information will help you to design a dwelling suitable for the area's conditions. The questions below will help you search for the right information. Look at books and magazines. Also, you may get useful help from people and companies who deal with energy, like gas and electricity. The Centre for Alternative Technology at Machynleth in Wales has lots of information about sensible ways of saving energy.

How hot does it become in summer?
How cold does it become in winter?
What is the average rainfall? Does rain vary from month to month?
Is the site exposed to a lot of wind? If so how could you use it?
Does a lot of snow fall?
Are there other problems like earthquakes or floods?
What modern technologies can be used to save energy on your site?
Are there traditional buildings on similar sites which have overcome some of these problems? How?

BUDGET

Usually practical tasks have to be done within a *fixed budget*. For example you might want to re-decorate your bathroom but only have £50 to do it with. The £50 is your *fixed* budget because you can spend no more.

In this task you will be allowed to spend up to 100 *World Bank Credits*. You can use this to buy building materials. Remember to plan your budget so that you do not run out of credits. The costs of the materials you might use are shown on the next two pages.

Location – Denmark
Nearest town – Varde
Place – River Varde
Geology – dry river bed
Base material – gravel

Location – Northern Italy
Nearest town – Cortina D'ampezzo
Place – Dolomites
Geology – mountain foothills
Base material – steep slope constructed from plaster

ENVIRONMENTS

Location – Canada
Nearest town – Toronto
Place – Lake Ontario
Geology – natural lake
Base material – water

Location – Republic of Ireland
Nearest town – Athlone
Place – marshland
Geology – peat marsh
Base material – saturated peat

Location – Western Europe
Nearest town – Esbjerg (50 miles east)
Place – North Sea
Geology – 50 metres below surface
Base material – rough water

Location – Western Australia
Nearest town – Jiggalong
Place – Gibson Desert
Geology – sandy desert
Base material – sand

MATERIALS

The materials in your school may not be exactly the same as those described here. You will not be using real building materials either. Your task is to design and make a *model* which looks as real as possible. The important things to consider are: dwelling layout; appearance; construction; and use of materials.

If you are able to use other materials, make sure you know what their *properties* are. This will help you to use them sensibly. *Properties* are the qualities a material has for example *waterproof*, *tough*, *colourful*, *light*, *easy to bend*, and so on.

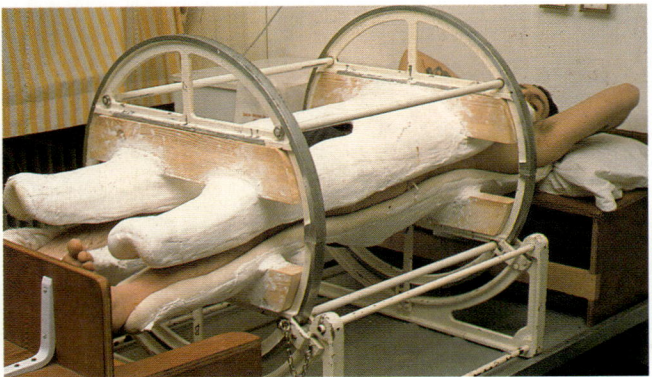

Modroc is a bandage which has plaster attached and is similar to the material used for plaster casts which are put on broken bones. After being softened in water for a few seconds it can be applied to frameworks where it sets 'like rock'.

* 50 credits per 300mm square

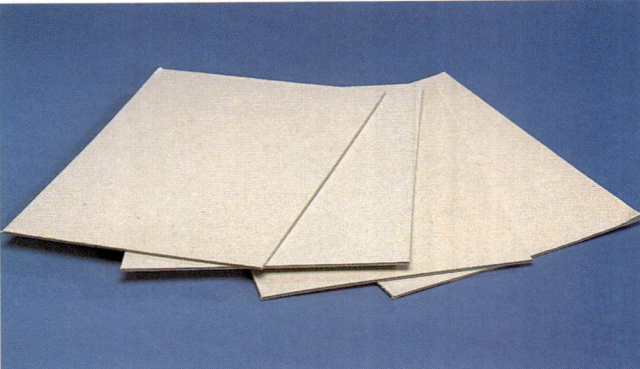

Greyboard is thick card. It is fairly cheap and ideal for constructing walls, roofs and room divisions. You can cut it with craft knives (be careful), scissors or a guillotine. It can be joined with PVA glue.

* 25 credits per 300mm square

Correx or corriflute is a plastic material which is built a little like corrugated cardboard. Because it is plastic it is waterproof but the open ends need to be sealed. It is light, strong, and colourful. Like greyboard it can be used for walls, roofs, and room divisions, but can be used in damp conditions. You can join it with a glue gun, or tabs and slots.

* 30 credits per 300mm square

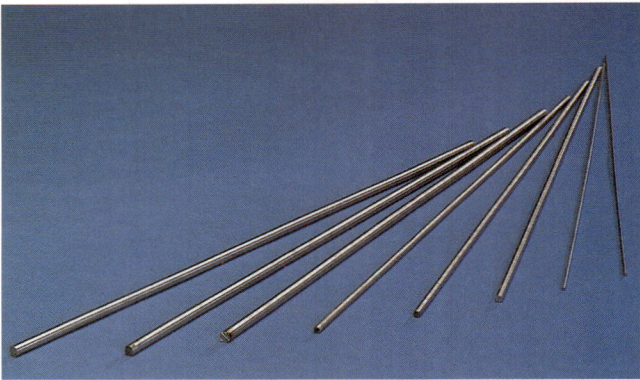

Wires and welding rods come in a variety of diameters. They are made of steel and are very tough. They can be bent to many shapes and soldered together. You can use both for frames and to represent things like pipes.

* Wire: 5 credits per 300mm length
  Welding rod: 5 credits per 150mm length

Balsa wood comes in many shapes and sizes. It is very light and strong but expensive. Because it is wood, it can be used to represent real wood in a dwelling. Join with balsa cement or a glue gun.

* Because of the wide range of shapes and sizes the cost will have to be decided by your teacher

Plastic bottles, like lemonade or washing up liquid can be used in various ways. Also, there may be other 'waste' objects which you may be able to make use of, like cardboard containers.

* If you get these yourself there will be no credit charge

Plywood is made from thin layers of wood glued together. The grain of the layers runs in alternate directions to make plywood strong and keep it flat. It comes in various thicknesses usually from 1.5mm to 25mm. Join with PVA or other woodworking glue.

* Because of the range of thicknesses and grades of plywood the cost will have to be decided by your teacher

Mirrorcard is a card with a mirror surface which reflects light. It comes in various colours, but is usually silver. Some types have a self adhesive back. You can join it with clear glue like Bostik or UHU or with PVA. It can be very useful to create the effect of solar panels.

* 50 credits per 300mm square

Modelling clay can be used when you need to mould more complicated shapes. It should not be applied too thickly otherwise it will crack as it dries. Plasticine is similar but more expensive.

* 30 credits per 500g

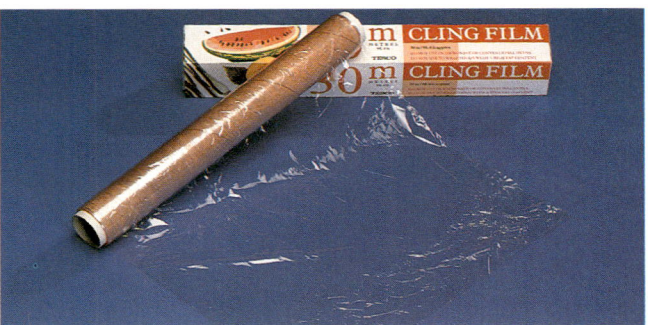

Clear plastic film (cling-film or similar) comes in rolls and will cling to other materials quite well. If you stretch it over an area, then heat it carefully with a hair dryer it will become tight.

* 20 credits per 300mm length

CONSTRUCTION TECHNIQUES

■ Cut thick card about half-way through before trying to bend it. This gives a neater bend.

■ Corners can be joined in card by using *folding tabs*. Glue these with PVA or a similar adhesive.

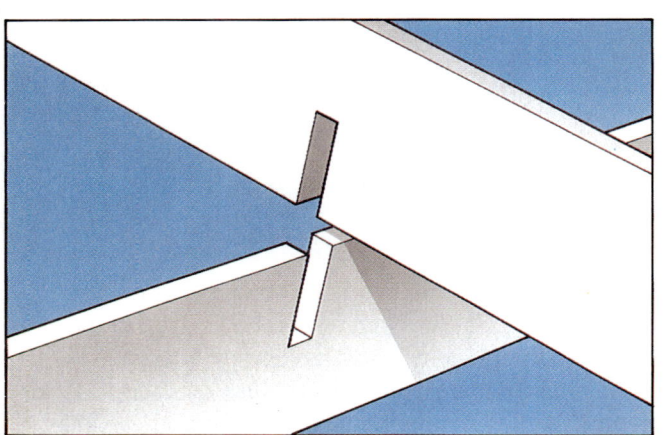

■ You can join pieces in the middle to make walls or floors. Cut slots halfway across. These are called *halving joints*.

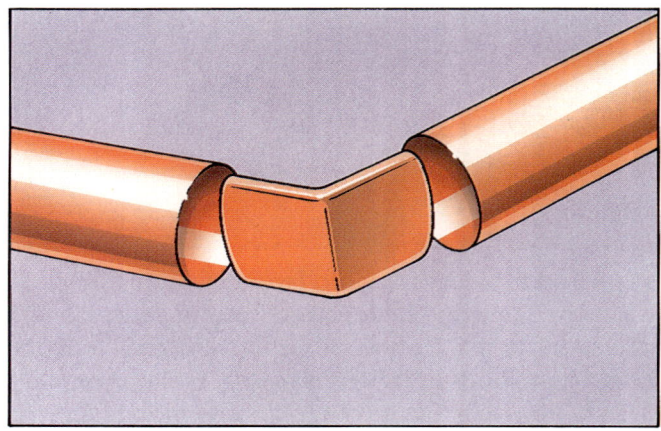

■ Joints can be *reinforced* on artstraws. Push short lengths of flattened straw into the joints with a little glue.

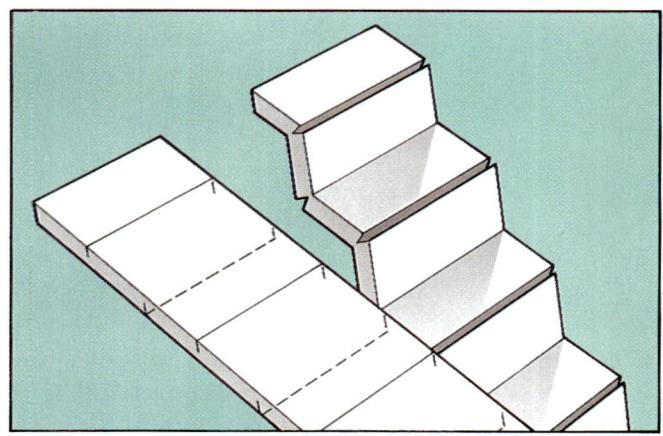

■ You can make stairs with thick card cut through on *alternate* sides and folded into shape.

■ Peel the top layer of corrugated cardboard to produce roof tiles.

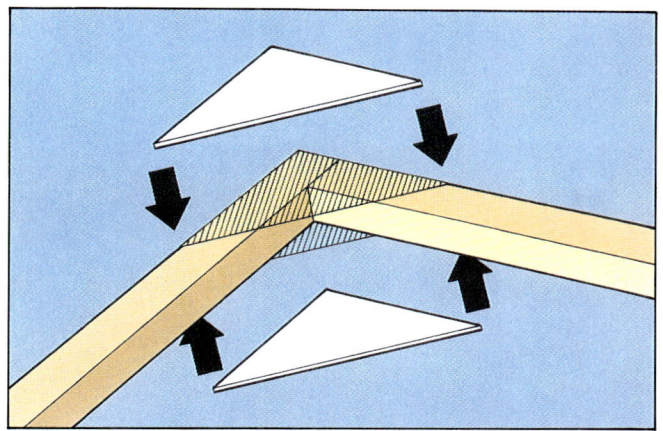

■ Reinforce balsa and other wooden frames at the corners with glued card triangles.

■ You can also do this when three pieces join together.

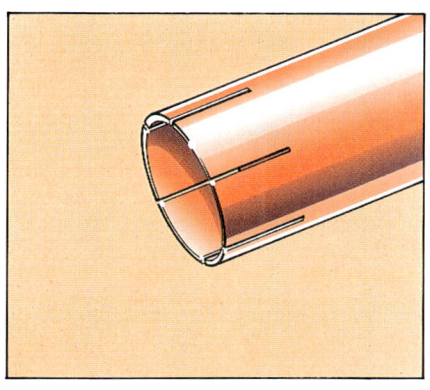

■ To fix artstraws to card try cutting down the straw a little way.

■ Then push the straw through a hole in the card (this can be made with a paper punch).

■ Bend the ends of the straws over and glue them to the back of the card.

■ Use waste objects or materials to make shapes which might be difficult with new materials.

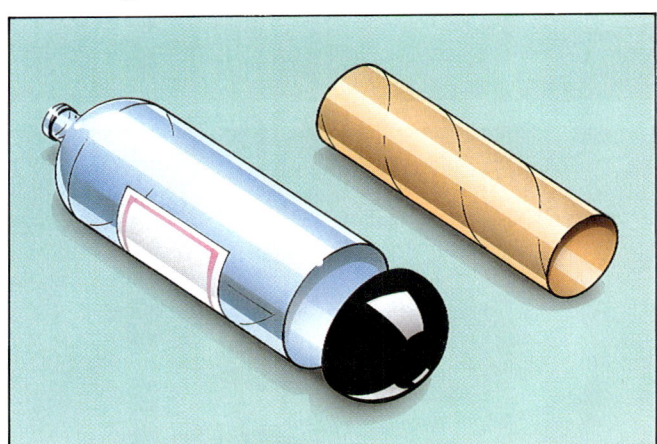

■ Cut the ends of plastic lemonade bottles to make domes.
■ Use kitchen roll centres to create interesting shapes.

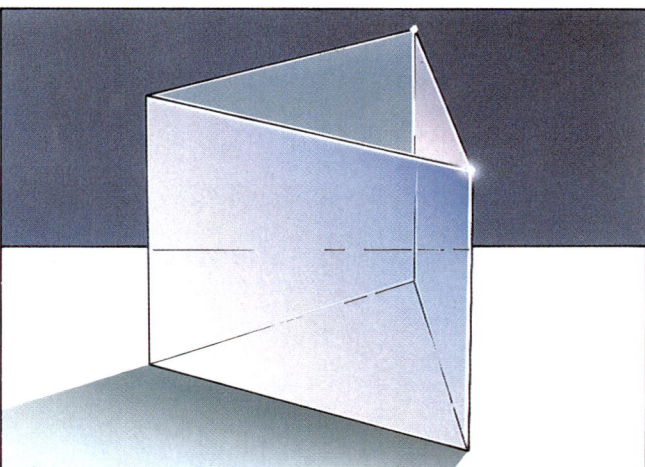

■ Rigid clear plastic can be formed into structures like greenhouses.
■ **Remember** to experiment until you get the effect you want. But do it *carefully* and when not sure ask your teacher.

INTO SPACE

It is now possible to live in space at least for a time. Astronauts either take enough supplies with them, or they are supplied from Earth. Yet it would be much easier to survive for long periods in space if astronauts could be self-sufficient; that is supplying all their own needs.

Space is short of two very important things we need to live: air and gravity.

◆ Find out how air is produced for space travellers at present. Could this be done for many thousands of travellers?

Gravity is a slightly different problem. Look at the fairground ride shown opposite. When it turns the riders are pushed against the wall. When the floor tilts they do not fall out but stay pinned against the wall. This is a type of artificial gravity. Using the same idea of spinning it may be possible to create artificial gravity in space. This would help astronauts overcome weightlessness. Two possible ways of doing this are shown below.

This spinning drum has large windows. Mirrors reflect sunlight through them. Opposite each window food is grown in artificial gardens.

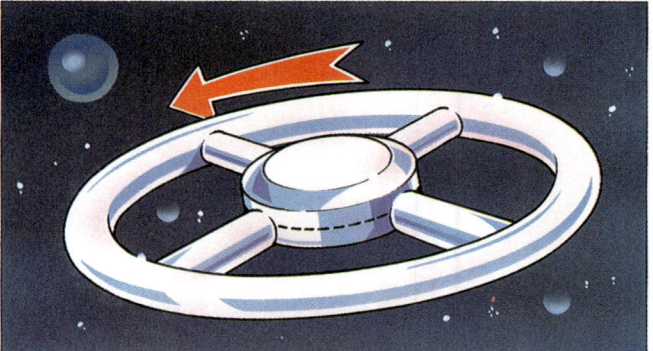

This design may well be a mile or more across the ring and would rotate once every minute.

DESIGN TASK: SPACE STATION

★ Design and make a model of a space station. You may need to make two models, one to show the overall idea and one to show the inside details.

● Begin by answering these questions.
What shapes could space stations be?
What things would the stations have to produce to be self-sufficient?
What benefits would living in space bring?

As you consider these questions you may form design ideas. Draw them in your design book. Here are some other ideas for you to examine.

■ Vacuum-formed panels all the same size could be linked together to form living *modules*.

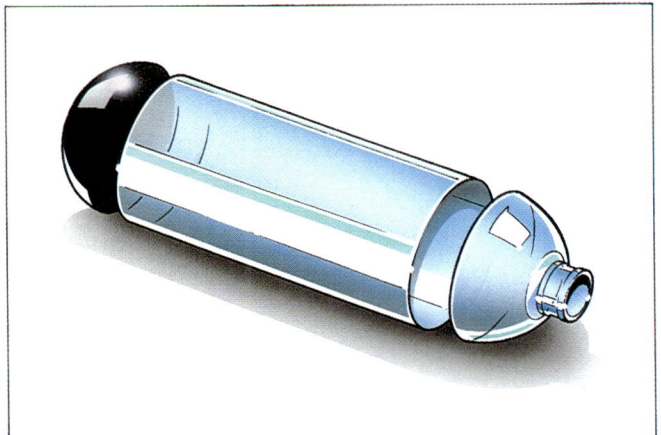

■ Plastic bottles or cardboard tubes could be your starting points for living accommodation.

■ Several tubes joined together could create the outer ring. Cutting parts of these away will help you show what is inside.

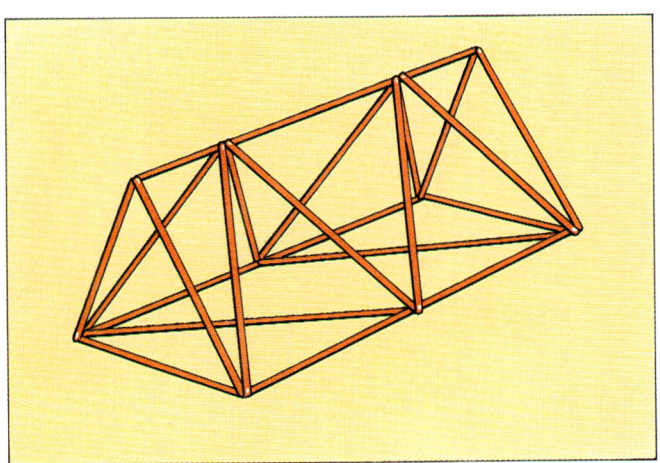

■ Artstraw structures may help you to link up parts of your space station. Why do you think these are best made up of triangles?

■ Your model might look effective against a background painted to look like space.

TO THE PLANETS

In time, people may *colonise* moons and planets. The planet Mars has a day 24½ hours long. It has seasons like Earth but no plant life. Because it is smaller than Earth its gravity is lower. The atmosphere is thinner and contains no free oxygen.

DESIGN TASK

★ Design and make a model of a settlement for a thousand people who will be living on Mars for a period of years.

◆ Begin by answering these questions.

1 What sort of minerals can be found on Mars?
2 How might settlers use them to make buildings and equipment?
3 How would a building on Mars differ from a space station?
4 What would a building on Mars have to do to protect people?
5 The first settlers on Mars might be scientists, technologists and miners. What facilities would they need for a comfortable life?

The atmosphere on Mars is thin and the planet is cold. The settlement will need some structures which trap the sun's rays. Perhaps large greenhouses will cover hundreds of acres. Inside will be a totally *artificial* atmosphere.

ESSENTIAL	NON-ESSENTIAL
Sleeping quarters	Discotheque

★ Make a list of the facilities the colonists would need. Divide the list into two columns in a table. The *essentials* are those things which the settlers could not do without. The *non-essentials* improve peoples' lives but they could do without them if they had to.

As you develop and sketch your designs think about the ideas shown on these pages.

Domes can be made in plastic sheet by blow moulding or vacuum forming. If you cannot do this, try papier mâché over a balloon. Tunnels can be made by cutting tubes in half.

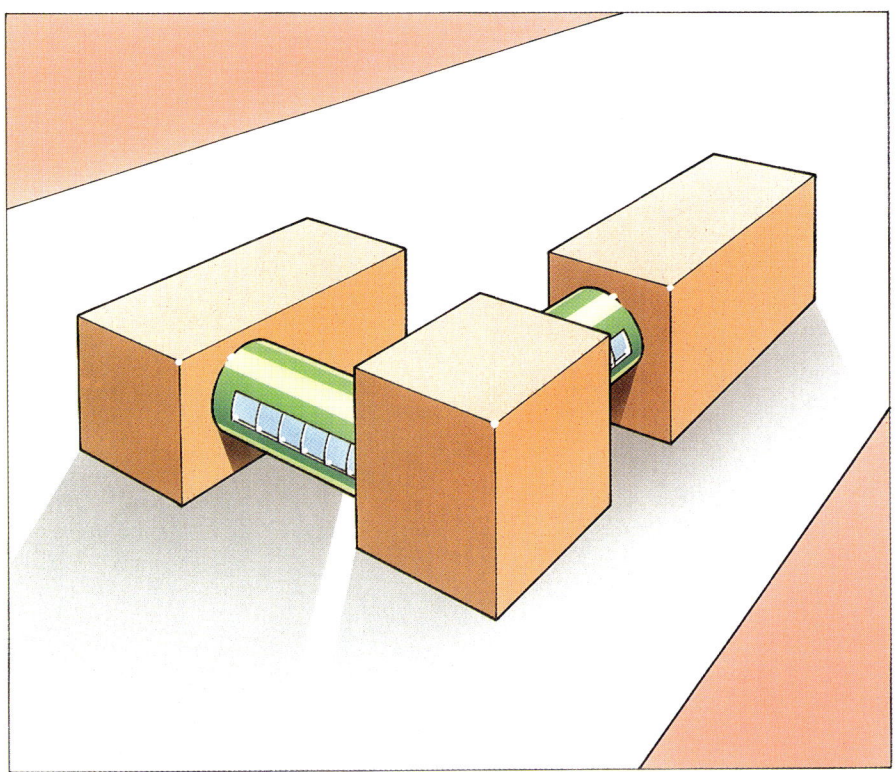

Rectangular blocks and hollow tubes make interesting settlements.

DESIGN TASK

★ Design and make a model vehicle to carry large cargoes across the surface of Mars.

★ After some time there may be many settlements scattered across Mars. Design and make a model of a *system* for carrying people between the settlements.

amplify

chips

communicate

satellite

transmit

inform

This section is about how we might communicate with each other in the future. It looks at how communications are improving and how satellites have helped. You will then be able to design and make a model of a futuristic personal communicator.

MESSAGES

SATELLITE COMMUNICATION

We are used to television programmes showing events, as they happen, right across the world. Speeches, rock performances, and sports can be seen at the same time by millions of people in many different countries. This is only possible because satellites relay the television broadcasts across vast distances in a split second.

Satellites can be placed in space to spin around the earth at the same speed as the Earth itself. This makes them hover over the same point on the Earth. We call this a *geostationary orbit*.

TELSTAR

The first communications satellite, Telstar was launched by the USA in 1962. It allowed a live link between the USA and the UK.

Television signals were sent to Telstar. Telstar then sent them back down to earth many miles from where they first came from. The signals from Telstar were very weak. They had to be received by a large dish and then *amplified* (increased) before being broadcast to ground televisions.

Before Telstar, television signals were sent along cables, or transmitted from aerials over short distances.

Television transmitters and aerials were placed as high as possible. If hills or tall buildings were in the way the signals were poor. The curve of the earth's surface also reduced distances that signals could travel. Communication satellites solve these problems.

Television signals from satellites give us a choice of programmes from all over Europe and further afield. Communcations satellites are now powerful enough to send signals right to our homes. All we need is a small satellite dish to receive the signals.

● Do you think the quality of television programmes will improve as we get more and more channels to choose from? Discuss this with your friends.

THE ELECTRONICS REVOLUTION

As electronics develop we can expect great changes in how we *communicate* with others.

Electronic circuits can store and process information. They are getting smaller all the time. The first electronic computers built in the 1950s filled whole rooms. Now, far more powerful computers sit on desk tops and hand-held computers will even fit into our pockets.

CHIPS

The introduction of *integrated circuits* has allowed computers to become so small. Every year new circuits (chips) are designed to cram more and more into less and less space.

DATA COMPRESSION

We can now also *compress* electronic information. The information can be transmitted in a short burst and stored. It can then be replayed at the right speed. This reduces transmission time which cuts the costs of satellite use.

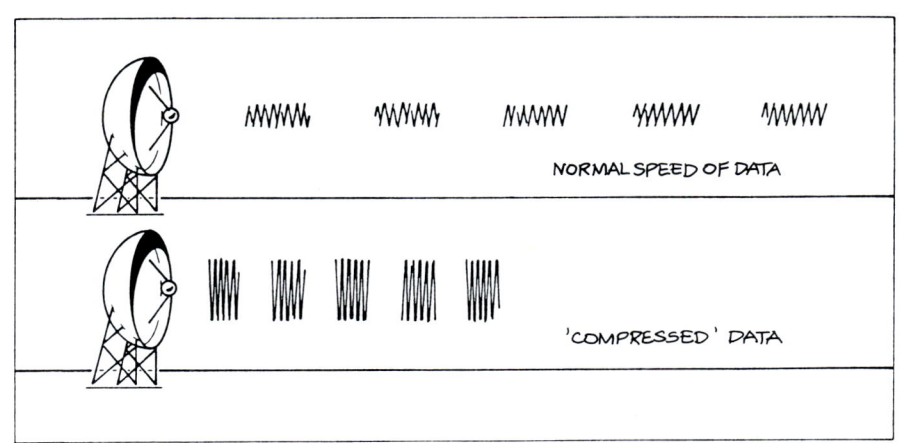

The recording and replaying of information has also lead to new technologies recently. Tape recorders have shrunk to Walkman size. LPs have reduced to compact discs and are still shrinking in diameter. Information can even be stored in integrated circuits and replayed without any mechanical moving parts.

Each generation of microchips becomes more powerful and uses less energy than the last.

A FUTURE COMMUNICATOR

A wide range of cellular phones is already in use. As technology improves the telephones get smaller and cheaper. At present they only work properly when close to a transmitter. This relays signals to the phones. Designers are working to improve cellular phones to spread their use more widely.

DESIGN TASK

★ Can you design a prototype model for the next generation of communications equipment?

Your task as a designer is to design and model a prototype personal communicator which builds on existing technology. Of course you are only going to make a model, not a real working communicator. However, your design should aim to do these jobs:

1 transmit and receive speech in all areas within range of communications satellites;
2 receive information which can then be stored and played back later on a data screen;
3 be light and small enough to fit into a jacket pocket.

■ Science fiction toys can be a source of good ideas for futuristic design.

DESIGN CONSIDERATIONS

1 The new generation of communications may use *data compression* methods. For your design assume that the unit shown below will be capable of data compression.

2 A small aerial or micro receiver dish may be needed. A microphone and sound generator will also be required to aid clear spoken sound.

3 Both the microphone and sound generator will work at low power. They will need to be held close to the mouth or ear when in use.

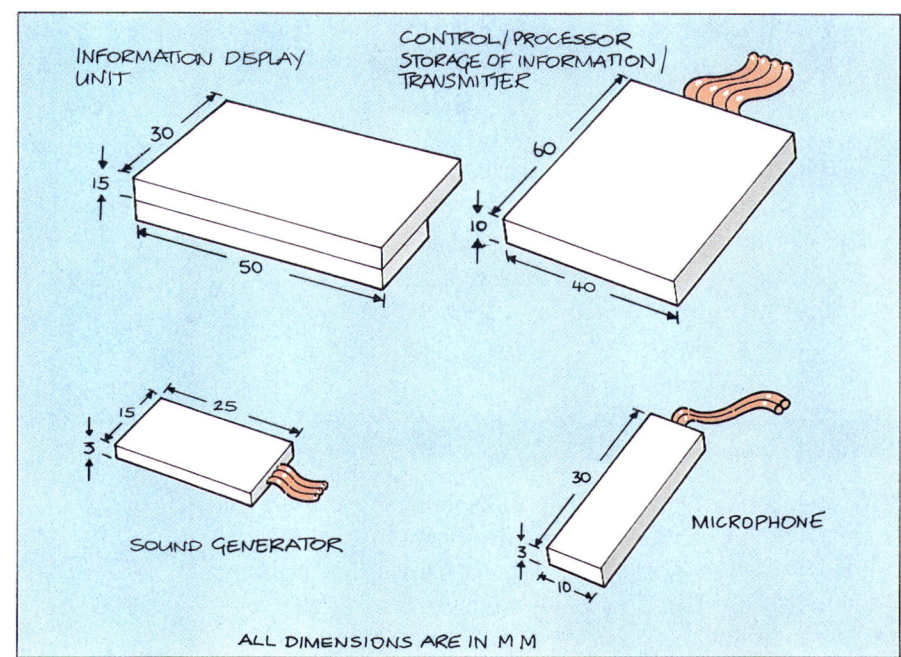

RESEARCH

◆ Think about the position of controls and other working parts. Work out how to make sure they are easy and safe to use.

Think about folding or extending parts of the communicator. This may reduce its size, or help protect some parts.

You also need to examine various ways of carrying and displaying the communictor for different uses.

How will the shape of your head influence the way you design the communicator?

DEVELOPMENT

★ Draw out your ideas. When you are ready make a *mock-up* (a quick model) using card or styrofoam. This will help you to test your ideas to see how they feel in use.

Ask yourself if your mock-up works well. If not how can it be improved? You might need to try a few ideas before you find the best solution.

PROTOTYPE MODEL

★ Finally make a *prototype model*. This should look and feel as real as you can make it. Try using *medium density fibreboard* or *jelutong*. Be careful to model the details such as screw heads, push buttons and display screens. You will find lots of tips in model making books. Work hard to get a good finish: *cellulose spray paint* will help you to do this.

WE CAN CHANGE THE FUTURE

There are many arguments over how we should plan to live in the future. Some people say that we can use science and technology to solve the problems of pollution or to create more food. Others argue that this approach has failed and that we should return to a simpler way of living that causes less damage to the environment.

A HIGH TECHNOLOGY FUTURE CITY

Our society has created much of its wealth from industrial manufacture. Large industrial cities, coal mines, and steel works have made a large impact on the environment. Increasingly we are using 'new technology' such as computers, biotechnology, lasers, and robots to produce the goods and services that we sell for profit. The new technology doesn't use the large amounts of raw materials required previously and appears to cause less damage. A better use of technology could enable safer atomic power plants, faster traffic through city centres, and improved electronic communications.

AN INTERMEDIATE TECHNOLOGY VILLAGE

This would use low-cost technology to cut the amount of gas and electricity bought in by the villagers.

- Household and animal waste is used to make bio-gas.
- The wind or a nearby river is used as a power source for electricity.
- Solar panels help to heat household water.
- House rubbish that burns is separated and used for fuel for heating houses.

● Debate the advantages and disadvantages of life in a hi-tech future city or intermediate technology village?

STARTING TO CHANGE THINGS OURSELVES

Many of the environmental problems we face are so large that we feel helpless and become concerned that we have nothing to offer. However, we can all make a practical contribution to improve our planet. The more ordinary people work together to change things for the better rather than pollute the environment, the sooner change will take place. As an individual you can make changes which will conserve energy, reduce the problems caused by household waste, and aid conservation!

MAJOR DESIGN TASKS

CONSERVATION

Conservationists examine the environment in which humans, birds, insects, and mammals make their homes. They look carefully at their needs for food, shelter, security, and generally how each species co-exists with others who share the same space. When conservationists understand the needs of the living things in an environment they can then propose changes which would bring about improvement. For example they could encourage mammals or birds to return to places they have previously abandoned.

◆ Find a small piece of waste land that you will be allowed to change and then carefully examine and record the plants and other inhabitants.

★ Make notes and sketches to show what changes you want to make, how they will be carried out, how much they will cost, and what improvements you can make.

▲ Observe and record the changes that take place over a period of time.

ENERGY

The consumption of oil, coal, and gas has risen steadily for many years as we use these sources of energy to heat and light our homes or for transport. These natural resources are rising in price as they become more difficult to find and the pollution caused when they are burned is also becoming an increasing problem. Many designers are trying to reduce the use of energy but there are still problems we can all help to solve.

◆ Find out what forms of fuel are available. Which are fossil fuels and which are renewable? Research how they can be conserved, used most effectively, and how consumption can be controlled.

★ Design a product, system, or campaign that will reduce the consumption of heat or light in the home or school.

▲ Recording the energy saved over a set period will help you measure how effective your design has been. Make sure any of the costs of your design changes are incorporated into your records.

RECYCLING

In Britain we produce mountains of household waste which has to be collected, carried long distances, and burned or dumped into enormous holes in the ground. Some of this waste can be re-cycled and used a second time, saving raw materials and energy, and reducing the bulk of the waste that has to be disposed of. Glass, aluminium, and paper are often found in household refuse and can each be reused after treatment.

◆ The key to re-cycling lies in the separation of the materials for reuse from the waste. Look carefully at how the materials can be separated, stored, transported, and treated before being reused. Local companies may be able to help with the prices of scrap materials.

★ Make drawings of a method or system that will help to sort, or in some other way ease, the recycling of household waste. Make a model if this will help.

▲ Record the time spent in the re-cycling along with the amount of the raw materials collected.

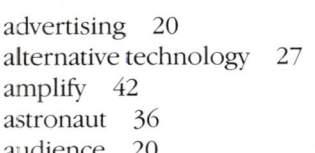

INDEX

advertising 20
alternative technology 27
amplify 42
astronaut 36
audience 20

back projection 19
badge 15
belt 13, 16
blow moulding 39
bracelet 14
budget 27

cellular phone 44
change 6, 46
climate 27
clothes 10, 11, 12, 13, 14, 16
communication 6, 9, 42, 44, 45
computer 8, 43
conservation 47

data compression 45
display 17
dwelling 27, 28, 31

electricity 27
electronics 43
energy 47
environment 28, 47
entertainment 16

fashion 6, 8, 10, 11, 12
finance 27
future 6, 8, 9, 10, 20, 41, 44

game 16

geology 27, 28
graphics 20, 21
gravity 36

headband 12
helmet 12

image 12, 14, 21
industry 46
integrated circuit 43
intermediate technology 46

jewellery 15

leisure 8, 10, 16
lettering 20
light-emitting diode (LED) 12, 15
lighting 19

materials 27, 32, 33
microchip 43
mock-up 45
money 78
movie 19

need 24, 38

plan 17
planets 38
playback 45
pollution 8, 24, 46, 47
power 28, 29
profit 20
programme 21
properties 32
props 18

prototype 45

receiver 45
recycling 47
robot 6

satellite 42, 44
self-sufficiency 27
shape 21
shelter 27
show 16
signal 11, 44
solar collector 27
space 24, 26, 36, 37
spectacles 12
storyboard 17
style 11
survival 16

technology 26, 43
television 42
Telstar 42
transmit 42, 43, 44
transport 18

use 27

vacuum forming 37, 39
visual impact 21

waste 27, 46, 47
wealth 46
work 8

Acknowledgements
The publishers wish to thank the following for permission to reproduce photographs:

Aspect Picture Library, pp 25 (top right, centre), 26 (bottom), 27 (left), 31 (bottom); **Barnaby's Picture Library**, pp 6 (top left), 10 (bottom left), 11 (left), 24 (right), 25 (top left), 27 (top left), 31 (bottom right, top left, top); **J Allan Cash**, pp 31 (top right), 36 (top); **Bruce Coleman**, pp 11 (left), 12 (centre), 27 (top right), 29 (left); **Hulton Picture Library**, p 6 (bottom left); **Image Bank**, pp 10 (top left), 11 (centre), 14 (left), 27 (centre); **I. Keill**, pp 6 (bottom right), 24 (left); **Photo Source**, pp 10 (top right), 43, 44; **Picturepoint**, pp 26 (left), 36 (top); **Science Photo Library**, pp 29 (bottom left), 43; **Telegraph Colour Library**, pp 6 (top right), 10 (bottom right), 12 (left), 14 (bottom left), 31 (left), 32; **Tropix Photo Library**, p. 29; **Wind Energy Group**, p 29; **Zefa Photographic Library**, p 12.

Additional photography by **Chris Honeywell**.

Illustrations by **Peter Campbell, Sarah Nicholson, Peter Owen, Lynne Riding**.

Oxford University Press, Walton Street, Oxford OX2 6DP

Oxford New York Toronto
Delhi Bombay Calcutta Madras Karachi
Petaling Jaya Singapore Hong Kong Tokyo
Nairobi Dar es Salaam Cape Town
Melbourne Auckland

and associated companies in
Berlin Ibadan

Oxford is a trade mark of Oxford University Press

© Anne Ablay, Peter Goulden, Neil Nuckley, Peter Toft.

ISBN 0 19 832780 3

Typeset in Garamond light & News Gothic by Tradespools Limited, Frome, Somerset
Printed in Hong Kong

First published 1990